I0785990

WEIRD PSYCHOLOGY

Truly Strange Findings of Science

By
Bradley W. Rasch

INTRODUCTION

To truly understand human behavior a basic knowledge of psychology and other sciences are important. This book will introduce you to some findings about human behavior and the science of psychology that will surprise you. You will learn about the accuracy of memory, and if it can change. You will find out why most psychological research is weird. You will finally discover if it is an advantage to be blonde. These and other strange discoveries will be found within the pages of this book.

TABLE OF CONTENTS

1
ALICE IN WONDERLAND

There is actually a psychological disorder called " Alice in Wonderland Syndrome". Specifically, it is a neurological disorder that causes a person to perceive themselves, or objects, as getting larger or smaller like the main character in Alice In Wonderland, by Lewis Carroll. Fortunately, this order is extremely rare, so rare that most psychologists have not heard of the term. The hallucinations are often preceded by an " Aura", much like migraine headaches are often preceded by an Aura. Interesting fact, Lewis Carroll suffered from migraines.

2
DOGS AND THEIR PEOPLE

Research has shown that many dogs do resemble their people. If you give pictures of dogs and pictures of their owners to a group of people that know neither the dog nor the owner, they are able to match them up with a stunning degree of accuracy. This also holds true with people and their cars.

For my midlife crisis, I went out and bought a Dachshund. It was one good-looking bitch.

3
BRAINS AND BASKETBALL

The great American Philosopher Yogi Berra once said, "Baseball is ninety percent **mental**. The other **half** is physical." Yogi was really on to something here. Yogi's wisdom extends to research conducted with professional basketball players.

Professional players can predict with a very high, almost perfect, degree of accuracy what balls are going in the exact moment the ball leaves the shooters hand. The superstars, i.e., the Michael Jordon's, can accurately predict balls going in *before* the ball leaves the shooters hand. Scientific research strongly suggests that elite players develop neuron pathways in their brains that allow them to accurately predict the actions of all the players on the court. In essence, the game " slows down" for the elite players.

4
SMILE!

The facial expressions we make impact our emotional state. We are actually happier if we smile. Folks that have Botox treatments for "frown lines" frequently report being happier. Some of the benefits of smiling:

You can build trust with a smile.

Studies have demonstrated that a sincere smile increases the trust that the receiver of that smile feels. The more pronounced your smile (not a silly smile, but a big genuine smile), the more others will trust you. Building trust is an absolute must in business and for individual success, and when you give customers a warm smile, they are much more likely to trust you.

Help your heart.

Smiling not only can relax your body, it also has the power to slow your heart rate, reduce blood pressure, and decrease the chances of heart disease.

Be more popular.

Most of us are hesitant to approach someone who is frowning, but we are naturally drawn to those who smile. Though this has been demonstrated, Jimmy Carter still lost to Ronald Reagan. Well.

Increase your positivity.

Those who smile often are significantly more likely to feel positive and content with their lives.

Increase your productivity.

Smiling can diminish negativity and boost your productivity. Research has demonstrated that a few minutes of smiling and laughter motivates people to work harder and can even enhance their creativity.

Appear more youthful.

People who smile appear more youthful. The muscles we use to smile lift our faces--no need for a face-lift, just smile more. When you smile, you are more attractive to others.

Find success by smiling.

When we smile at others we show confidence. Studies have found that those who smile frequently make more money in tips, are much more likely to receive a raise, and more likely to be promoted compared with their frowning peers.

Become the best leader you can be.

Studies have proved that smiling is an effective leadership technique. Colleagues are more receptive to leaders who smile--begin and end a request with a friendly smile.

Lower stress and improve your mood.

Too much stress can be a causative factor for a host of problems, including, but not limited to, obesity, asthma, headaches, Alzheimer's disease, and even premature death. Smiling reduces your stress and cuts your risk of these stress-related risks. It improves your mood significantly, as well as that of others who are lucky enough to witness your smile.

Improves your immune system.

Smiling and its relaxing help amp up your immune system. Smile more to ward off illnesses and stay healthy.

Pain reduction.

The release of neurotransmitters that come from smiling acts as a natural painkiller.

Longer Life

Some studies have suggested that you can add some years to your life by smiling often.

Be an evangelist for happiness.
Your smile can lighten the mood of any situation your find yourself in. Research shows smiles can be contagious. Bring more happiness to the world--greet everyone with a smile.

"A smile is an inexpensive way to change your looks".
-- Charles Gordy

5
LAUGH!

Laughter has its origins long before humor. It has long served as a social cue that allows others to know we like them or are comfortable with them. So laughter serves the same social purpose for humans as tailing wagging for dogs.

Statistically, people laugh at things that are not funny more than they laugh at statements that can be considered funny.

Laughter provides many health benefits:

1. Laughter reduces physical tension and stress.
2. Laughter enhances your immune system.
3. Laughter actually improves your mood, and that improvement can be contagious in a social situation.
4. Laughter can decrease your odds of contracting heart disease.
5. Laughter allows you to look at issues differently; it allows you to see things through the eyes of others.
6. There are social benefits to laughter. Others perceive you as being nicer and more approachable. People are more at ease around you.

"[Humanity] has unquestionably one really effective weapon—laughter. Power, money, persuasion, supplication, persecution—these can lift at a colossal humbug—push it a little—weaken it a little, century by century, but only laughter can blow it to rags and atoms at a blast. Against the assault of laughter nothing can stand". — Mark Twain

6
TICKLE!

No one can tickle him or herself. When you move an arm, the brain sends out a message to move the arm. A "shadow message" (called a corollary discharge) is also sent out and predicts your movement and tampers down your senses. This is a way your brain allows you to differentiate between your internal experience and the experience you have with the outside world. You cannot, in essence, surprise your self.

Schizophrenics can, however, tickle themselves.

7
IT'S NOT ALL BLACK AND WHITE

Psychological researchers have a test that they use called the Implicit Association Test. This test can accurately measure how quickly we make associations with words that are flashed on a screen rapidly. Multiple experiments have consistently shown that sports fans required more time to come up with a positive adjective when shown the name of a player from a rival team. Also, white folks, even those that do not report themselves as being prejudiced, took longer to produce positive attributes about black people. They identified positive words about white people quicker.

8
MEMORIES

Memories are not always accurate. Why is that? Memories are stored in multiple parts of the brain. They are webs that are interconnected. When we remember something sometimes we add to it. We embellish it. This new memory may not be so accurate. Each time we revisit the memory of an event, we can change that memory. Next time you watch a legal drama and an eyewitness is testifying, *remember* this.

9
REALLY, LAUGH!

Laughing and smiling developed in human beings as a way of warding off aggression from others. Smiling at an aggressor is a way of letting that person know that you do not pose a threat to them. Laughing also wards off aggression. Approach a young infant with intent to tickle, the child will laugh before you tickle her. This is an instinctual defensive way of the child saying, " I pose no threat to you, and this is all fun and games".

10
LAUGH SOME MORE

Research has shown that you can increase productivity by getting workers to laugh. When faced with a boring manufacturing task, work volume increases when you show workers a funny video that prompts the person to laugh. To some degree, it appears humor in the workplace improves productivity.

Though there is no research on this, the author suggests that giving a slide presentation on your vacation probably decreases productivity and workplace morale.

11
MULTI-TASKING? THINK AGAIN!

Sitting at your desk at work, handling a call, reading a report, eating lunch, and watching the flat screen television way over in the break room. Wow, you are productive! Wrong. Multi-tasking may look impressive, but it is not. Those that multi-task do not get more work completed, and the work they do complete has a higher rate of errors. Find another way to impress the boss or look busy. A great deal of recent research suggests that multi-tasking is not a good thing. Lin Xie conducted the first research completed on this topic over five hundred years ago. He asked people to draw a circle with one hand and a square with the other simultaneously. The results were not pretty. They were, however, when the tasks were completed one at a time.

Do not do two things at the same time if you can avoid it. Gum chewing while you work is okay, however, unless you are in Ms. Van Kampama's Language Arts class.

12
IT WASN'T FREUD

Ask most people who "invented" psychology and they are likely to answer Sigmund Freud, arguably the most famous name in psychology other than Bradley Rasch.

Wilhelm Wundt, however, is really recognized as the " Father of Psychology". Wundt, 1832-1920 merged the disciplines of philosophy and physiology and established the first department of psychology at a university, the first psychological research laboratory, the first professional research journal in the field, and popularized the term psychology.

The bearded one many think invented the field did make some contributions. A little trivia about Freud: he not only used cocaine, but worked very hard to popularize it's "medicinal" use in medicine. He is best known for interpreting dreams and coining such terms as " penis envy".

Wundt, however, is known for insisting that the new field of psychology follow the scientific method and he insured that it became a " hard" science.

13
WAX NASTOLGIC

Feeling a little unhappy? Got some serious blues going on?
Look at some old photos from a happy time. Remember a long
ago vacation and talk about it. Recall a favorite song from your
youth. Fond memories, and sharing those memories, can uplift
your mood, and even enhance your self-esteem. That two-yard
run may become a seventy-yard touchdown at the state
championship in the retelling. Why not? It was forty years
ago, no one will remember and you will feel better. Maybe you
can pursue a career as a politician.

14
WAX AGAIN

Waxing nostalgic not only improves ones mood, but can help you feel better physically as well. When it is uncomfortably cold out, memories are triggered. " Warm" memories or listening to a favorite song from long ago can increase our body temperature.

15
YAK AWAY

The more you communicate with your children, the better
their vocabulary will be. One of the best predictors of a child's
language development is how much time their parent interacts
with them. Well-spoken children (and adults) are generally
perceived as being brighter. Vocabulary at age three
accurately predicts vocabulary at age ten. Good ten-year-old
communicators with impressive vocabularies are generally
very articulate adults.

So, yak away, but do so with quality communication,
expressing *and* listening.

16
TRAUMA?

Something bad happens to person A, the same exact thing happens to person B. To A, it is a traumatic event. To B, it is quickly forgotten. Why is that?

When something happens to us, we put a label on it: funny, terrible, scary, important, unimportant, etc, the label we put on it determines how we experienced the event.

One High School Freshman drops her books in the hallway at changing time. Oh, the embarrassment! Everyone notices and thinks I am a klutz!! We have to move to another community. This was a tragedy!!

Another student drops her books and simply forgets it happened. She never told herself it was a big deal. The label we choose to put on an event, to a large degree, determines what kind of event it was for us.

17
RESILIENCE

When discussing resilience, it is important to define it, illustrate it's importance, and discuss how one can build it.

Psychological resilience is defined as an individual's ability to successfully adapt to life tasks in the face of social disadvantage or other highly adverse conditions. Adversity and stress can come in the shape of family or relationship problems, health problems, or workplace and financial worries, among others.

Emotional resilience simply refers to one's ability to adapt to stressful. situations or crises. More **resilient** people are able to "roll with the punches" and adapt to adversity without lasting difficulties, while less **resilient** people have a harder time with stress and life change or challenges.

Many of these skills can be developed and strengthened, which can improve your ability to deal with life's setbacks. **Resilient** people are aware of situations, their own emotional reactions and the behavior of those around them. ... Another **characteristic of resilience** is the understanding that life is full of challenges, and always will be.

Resilience is the process of adapting well in the face of adversity, trauma, tragedy, threats or significant sources of stress — such as family and relationship problems, serious health problems or workplace and financial stressors. It means, "bouncing back" from difficult experiences.

Research has shown that resilience is ordinary, not extraordinary. People commonly demonstrate resilience. One example is the response of many Americans to the September 11, 2001 terrorist attacks and individuals' efforts to rebuild their lives.

Being resilient does not mean that a person doesn't experience difficulty or distress. Emotional pain and sadness are common in people who have suffered major adversity or trauma in their lives. In fact, the road to resilience is likely to involve considerable emotional distress.

Resilience is not a trait that people either have or do not have. It involves behaviors, thoughts and actions that can be learned and developed in anyone.

TEN WAYS TO BUILD RESILIENCE

Make connections. Good relationships with close family members, friends or others are important. Accepting help and support from those who care about you and will listen to you strengthens resilience. Some people find that being active in civic groups, faith-based organizations, or other local groups provides social support and can help with reclaiming hope. Assisting others in their time of need also can benefit the helper.

Avoid seeing crises as insurmountable problems. You can't change the fact that highly stressful events happen, but you can change how you interpret and respond to these events. Try looking beyond the present to how future circumstances may be a little better. Note any subtle ways in which you might already feel somewhat better as you deal with difficult situations.

Accept that change is a part of living. Certain goals may no longer be attainable as a result of adverse situations. Accepting circumstances that cannot be changed can help you focus on circumstances that you can alter.

Move toward your goals. Develop some realistic goals. Do something regularly — even if it seems like a small accomplishment — that enables you to move toward your goals. Instead of focusing on tasks that seem unachievable, ask yourself, "What's one thing I know I can accomplish today that helps me move in the direction I want to go?"

Take decisive actions. Act on adverse situations as much as you can. Take decisive actions, rather than detaching completely from problems and stresses and wishing they would just go away.

Look for opportunities for self-discovery. People often learn something about themselves and may find that they have grown in some respect as a result of their struggle with loss. Many people who have experienced tragedies and hardship have reported better relationships, greater sense of strength even while feeling vulnerable, increased sense of self-worth, a more developed spirituality and heightened appreciation for life.

Nurture a positive view of yourself. Developing confidence in your ability to solve problems and trusting your instincts helps build resilience.

Keep things in perspective. Even when facing very painful events, try to consider the stressful situation in a broader context and keep a long-term perspective. Avoid blowing the event out of proportion.

Maintain a hopeful outlook. An optimistic outlook enables you to expect that good things will happen in your life. Try visualizing what you want, rather than worrying about what you fear.

Take care of yourself. Pay attention to your own needs and feelings. Engage in activities that you enjoy and find relaxing. Exercise regularly. Taking care of yourself helps to keep your mind and body primed to deal with situations that require resilience.

Additional ways of strengthening resilience may be helpful. For example, some people write about their deepest thoughts and feelings related to trauma or other stressful events in their life. Meditation and spiritual practices help some people build connections and restore hope.
The key is to identify ways that are likely to work well for you as part of your own personal strategy for fostering resilience.

In short, resilience is knowing you have faced adversity before that you have dealt with it successfully, and will do so again.

The interesting thing about resilience, and researching it, is that it cannot be studied or assessed in the absence of tragedy. Until you are faced with a difficult situation, you will not know how resilient you are.

18
TOO MUCH TO SEE, TOO LITTLE TIME

More than ever before in human history, we have more information than we know what to do with. We have so many options to consider. If you want to make a purchase, you not only have countless options, but limitless information available to research before making a decision. As a result, our attention has become a valuable commodity to others.

Orange Juice in Denmark, Why Americans Are So Unhappy
Is an excellent book that discusses the pressures involved in having too many choices and too much information, and it's impact on our contentment.

19
PUT DOWN THAT PHONE

Research has shown that Eighty-Nine percent of cell phone users have used their cell phones during their most recent social interaction with others. What a great message to send the people you are with- you are not interesting enough or important enough to keep my attention during our forty-five minute lunch date. Really now?

The author taught college psychology for over thirty years, both before and during the cell phone era. One student was asked on several occasions not to text (or even receive calls) during lectures, as other students had complained. The instructor (your author) notified the student the next phone usage during class time would result in dismissal from the course. The next class, he made several texts, and took a call. He was notified that he was out of the course. He requested an appeal. During the appeal he received a text and responded to it.

In the early days of the ubiquitous smart phone psychologists speculated that intensive use of the device was due to FOMO (Fear of Missing Out). We know now that for some, smart phone use is addicting, the same areas of the brain are activated that are activated by some drug use. This is a real problem for many.

Some people have attended rehab for phone addiction.

Be aware of your own phone use. Does it make it appear as though you do not value the people you are actually with? Is your time on the device excessive in your opinion, or the opinion of others.

20
CAPGRAS, ANYONE?

Yes, this is a real psychological term. And, yes, it is included in this book because it has an odd sounding name, and a name you have probably never heard.

Capgras Syndrome is a real psychological disorder. Those that suffer from it believe that an imposter has replaced someone close to them.

21
WHY DID I COME TO THIS ROOM?

Have you ever walked into a room and forgotten why you were there? Welcome to my life. I have been doing this since I was a teenager. Thankfully, now I can call it a senior moment. I just called it being a Dofus when I was a kid.

Admit it. This has happened to you. Young, old, or in between, you have done this. Be not ashamed loyal reader, as this benign phenomenon shall be explained.

Now, what were we talking about? Oh, yes, forgetting why you walked into the room. Right?

Psychology has a name for this (actually two names):
" Doorway Effect" or " Location Updating Effect". My daughters also have a name for it: Dad.

This common problem occurs when our brains try to take in details of our new surroundings. Our brains record in segments, not in a continual loop, and it builds a little " mental divider" between our experiences of the two rooms. That natural divider disrupts the connections composing our memory, so that anything on the other side becomes more difficult.

Have you ever Just looked at your watch to see the time, and someone immediately asks you what time it is, and you have to look at your watch again? Same thing. In this case you were looking for the time for you, and not for them. You look at your watch the second time, about a second later, for them.

"As I was walking down the street one day
A man came up to me and asked me what
The time was that was on my watch, yeah... And I said

(I don't) Does anybody really know what time it is
(Care) Does anybody really care (about time)
If so I can't imagine why (Oh no, no)
We've all got time enough to cry"-Chicago

22
SCHIZOPHRENIA TREATMENT

Diagnosis of Schizophrenia

The DSM 5 (what psychologists and psychiatrists use to diagnose mental illness) outlines the following criterion to make a diagnosis of schizophrenia:

1. Two or more of the following for at least a one-month (or longer) period of time, and at least one of them must be 1, 2, or 3:

- Delusions
- Hallucinations
- Disorganized speech
- Grossly disorganized or catatonic behavior
- Negative symptoms, such as diminished emotional expression

1. Impairment in one of the major areas of functioning for a significant period of time since the onset of the disturbance: Work, interpersonal relations, or self-care.

2. Some signs of the disorder must last for a continuous period of at least 6 months. This six-month period must include at least one

month of symptoms (or less if treated) that meet criterion A (active phase symptoms) and may include periods of residual symptoms. During residual periods, only negative symptoms may be present.

3. Schizoaffective disorder and bipolar or depressive disorder with psychotic features have been ruled out:

- No major depressive or manic episodes occurred concurrently with active phase symptoms
- If mood episodes (depressive or manic) have occurred during active phase symptoms, they have been present for a minority of the total duration of the active and residual phases of the illness.

1. The disturbance is not caused by the effects of a substance or another medical condition

2. If there is a history of autism spectrum disorder or a communication disorder (childhood onset), the diagnosis of schizophrenia is only made if prominent delusions or hallucinations, along with other symptoms, are present for at least one month

Associated Features

There are a number of symptoms that contribute to a diagnosis of schizophrenia.

- Inappropriate affect (laughing in the absence of a stimulus)
- Disturbed sleep pattern
- Dysphoric mood (can be depression, anxiety, or anger)
- Anxiety and phobias
- Depersonalization (detachment or feeling of disconnect from self)
- Derealization (a feeling that surrounding aren't real)
- Cognitive deficits impacting language,

processing, executive
function, and/or
memory
- Lack of insight into
disorder
- Social cognition deficits
- Hostility and aggression

Cognitive impairments caused by the disorder may persist when other symptoms are in remission. This contributes to impairments in functioning in employment, interpersonal relationships, and the ability to engage in proper self-care.

Suicide risk

5%-6% of people with schizophrenia die by suicide, about 20% make suicide attempts on more than one occasion, and many more have significant suicidal thoughts. Suicidal behavior can be in response to hallucinations and suicide risk remains high over the lifespan of individuals with schizophrenia.

Functional consequences

Schizophrenia is associated with social and occupational dysfunction. Completing education and maintaining employment are negatively impacted by symptoms of the illness, and most individuals diagnosed with schizophrenia are employed at a lower level than their parents. Many have few or limited social relationships outside of their immediate family.

Diagnosis of Autism
Diagnostic Criteria
A.   Persistent difficulties in the social use of verbal and nonverbal communication as manifested by all of the following:

1.   Deficits in using communication for social purposes, such as greeting and sharing information, in a manner that is appropriate for the social context.

2.   Impairment of the ability to change communication to match context or the needs of the listener, such as speaking differently in a classroom than on the playground, talking differently to a child than to an adult, and avoiding use of overly formal language.

3.   Difficulties following rules for conversation and storytelling, such as taking turns in conversation, rephrasing when misunderstood, and knowing how to use verbal and nonverbal signals to regulate interaction.

4.   Difficulties understanding what is not explicitly stated (e.g., making inferences) and nonliteral or ambiguous meanings of language (e.g., idioms, humor, metaphors, multiple meanings that depend on the context for interpretation).

B.   The deficits result in functional limitations in effective communication, social participation, social relationships, academic achievement, or occupational performance, individually or in combination.

C.   The onset of the symptoms is in the early developmental period (but deficits may not become fully manifest until social communication demands exceed limited capacities).

D.   The symptoms are not attributable to another medical or neurological condition or to low abilities in the domains or word structure and grammar, and are not better explained by autism spectrum disorder, intellectual disability (intellectual developmental disorder), global developmental delay, or another mental disorder.
Autism Spectrum Disorder
Diagnostic Criteria

A.   Persistent deficits in social communication and social interaction across multiple contexts, as manifested by the following, currently or by history (examples are illustrative, not exhaustive, see text):
> 1.   Deficits in social-emotional reciprocity, ranging, for example, from abnormal social approach and failure of normal back-and-forth conversation; to reduced sharing of interests, emotions, or affect; to failure to initiate or respond to social interactions.
> 2.   Deficits in nonverbal communicative behaviors used for social interaction, ranging, for example, from poorly integrated verbal and nonverbal communication; to abnormalities in eye contact and body language or deficits in understanding and use of gestures; to a total lack of facial expressions and nonverbal communication.
> 3.   Deficits in developing, maintaining, and understanding relationships, ranging, for example, from difficulties adjusting behavior to suit various social contexts; to difficulties in sharing imaginative play or in making friends; to absence of interest in peers.
> *Specify* current severity:

Severity is based on social communication impairments and restricted repetitive patterns of behavior (see Table 2).

B.   Restricted, repetitive patterns of behavior, interests, or activities, as manifested by at least two of the following, currently or by history (examples are illustrative, not exhaustive; see text):

1.   Stereotyped or repetitive motor movements, use of objects, or speech (e.g., simple motor stereotypes, lining up toys or flipping objects, echolalia, idiosyncratic phrases).

2.   Insistence on sameness, inflexible adherence to routines, or ritualized patterns or verbal nonverbal behavior (e.g., extreme distress at small changes, difficulties with transitions, rigid thinking patterns, greeting rituals, need to take same route or eat food every day).

3.   Highly restricted, fixated interests that are abnormal in intensity or focus (e.g., strong attachment to or preoccupation with unusual objects, excessively circumscribed or preservative interest).

4.   Hyper- or hypo reactivity to sensory input or unusual interests in sensory aspects of the environment (e.g., apparent indifference to pain/temperature, adverse response to specific sounds or textures, excessive smelling or touching of objects, visual fascination with lights or movement).

Specify current severity:

Severity is based on social communication impairments and restricted, repetitive patterns of behavior (see Table 2).

C.   Symptoms must be present in the early developmental period (but may not become fully manifest until social demands exceed limited capacities, or may be masked by learned strategies in later life).

D.   Symptoms cause clinically significant impairment in social, occupational, or other important areas of current functioning.

E.   These disturbances are not better explained by intellectual disability (intellectual developmental disorder) or global developmental delay. Intellectual disability and autism spectrum disorder frequently co-occur; to make co morbid diagnoses of autism spectrum disorder and intellectual disability, social communication should be below that expected for general developmental level.

Note: Individuals with a well-established DSM-IV diagnosis of autistic disorder, Asperger's disorder, or pervasive developmental disorder not otherwise specified should be given the diagnosis of autism spectrum disorder. Individuals, who have marked deficits in social communication, but whose symptoms do not otherwise meet criteria for autism spectrum disorder, should be evaluated for social (pragmatic) communication disorder.

Specify if:

With or without accompanying intellectual impairment with or without accompanying language impairment Associated with a known medical or genetic condition or environmental factor

(**Coding note:** Use additional code to identify the associated medical or genetic condition.)

Associated with another neurodevelopmental, mental, or behavioral disorder

(**Coding note:** Use additional code[s] to identify the associated neurodevelopmental, mental, or behavioral disorder[s].)
With catatonia (refer to the criteria for catatonia associated with another mental disorder, pp. 119-120, for definition) (**Coding note:** Use additional code 293.89 [F06.1] catatonia associated with autism spectrum disorder to indicate the presence of the comorbid catatonia.)

Severity levels for autism spectrum disorder

Severity level	Social communication	Restricted, repetitive behaviors
Level 3 "Requiring very substantial support"	Severe deficits in verbal and nonverbal social communication skills cause severe impairments in functioning, very limited initiation of social interactions, and minimal response to social overtures from others. For example, a person with few words of intelligible speech who rarely initiates interaction and, when he or she does, makes unusual approaches to meet needs only and responds to only very direct social approaches	Inflexibility of behavior, extreme difficulty coping with change, or other restricted/repetitive behaviors markedly interfere with functioning in all spheres. Great distress/difficulty changing focus or action.
Level 2 "Requiring substantial support"	Marked deficits in verbal and nonverbal social communication skills; social	Inflexibility of behavior, difficulty coping with change, or other restricted/repetitive

	impairments apparent even with supports in place; limited initiation of social interactions; and reduced or abnormal responses to social overtures from others. For example, a person who speaks simple sentences, whose interaction is limited to narrow special interests, and how has markedly odd nonverbal communication.	behaviors appear frequently enough to be obvious to the casual observer and interfere with functioning in a variety of contexts. Distress and/or difficulty changing focus or action.
Level 1 "Requiring support"	Without supports in place, deficits in social communication cause noticeable impairments. Difficulty initiating social interactions, and clear examples of atypical or unsuccessful response to social overtures of others. May appear to have decreased interest in social interactions. For example, a person who is able to speak in full sentences and engages in communication but whose to- and-fro conversation with others fails, and whose attempts to make friends are odd and	Inflexibility of behavior causes significant interference with functioning in one or more contexts. Difficulty switching between activities. Problems of organization and planning hamper independence.

typically unsuccessful.

 Here is the interesting thing about the treatment of schizophrenia: Because schizophrenia and autism are at opposite ends of the Diametric Model of Mental Illness, one possible way to treat schizophrenia is to help schizophrenics become more autistic. There are certainly other methods of treatment, but this is an interesting concept.

23
AUTISM BENEFITS

There are a number of studies that have estimated that one-third of people with autism spectrum disorder have perfect pitch. A definite advantage for serious musicians and composers.

24
TONE AND MOODS

In a study of moods, subjects (participants) read aloud stories. Their voices were changed to sound happy, sad, or neutral. Their emotions were found to match the tone of their voices. Important to know when you are interacting with others, and others are sizing you up. It also demonstrates the frequent misleading that must be a part of social psychological research.

25
MISSING THE GYM?

Approximately eighty percent of people that have gym memberships do not use them. Though the following statement has not been researched, the author has noticed that those that have made New Years resolutions seem to come in January, but the gym seems a bit empty by February.

Why is this? Our will power is lessened by something called ego depletion. We have a limited amount of willpower, and it is depleted with overuse. When ego depletion comes into play, we loose self-control and self-esteem. When ego depletion happens, we often find ourselves in a bad mood.

26
HOW FAR IS THAT?

Folks that suffer from obesity tend to judge distances as being greater than they are. Our estimate of a distance is impacted by how much energy and effort it will take for us to get there.

Even more interesting: our perception of our body size had no impact on our ability to estimate distance. Our actual body weight is what impacts our ability to perceive distance accurately.

27
I'LL HAVE DESSERT!

Want that dessert? What factors make it more likely you will order it? Is it one of your favorites? Did you have a rough day, and believe you deserve a little luxury? Turns out neither one of these factors are a determinant. If your waiter or waitress is overweight, you are up to four times more likely to order dessert. You are also somewhat more likely to order alcohol. The thinner the diner is, the more impact the servers weight has on the diner's likelihood to order dessert.

I'll have that cheesecake, please.

28
REWARDS

We all know what "operant conditioning" is (researched by BF Skinner) whether we know it or not.

Want your dog to do its "business" outside? You give it a treat when it does. You "catch" your son sharing a toy with his younger brother, and you praise him profusely.

Do these things, or something like them? Then you understand operant conditioning, or what is often called rewards.

Research shows that behavior is often a result of its consequences. To an experimental psychologist a reward increases the frequency of events that it immediately follows.

29
RATS, SALAVATING DOGS, AND THE DENTIST

Ivan Pavlov is known for his salivating dogs. He is recognized as being one of the most important psychologists of all time (Little known fact: he was not a psychologist).

Pavlov knew dogs would salivate when they saw food. They did not have to learn this, they just did. He rang bells every time food was presented. Soon, the dogs learned to salivate when the bell was rung, even if food was not there. Because the food had been paired with the bells so often. Today we call this classical conditioning, or Pavlovian conditioning in honor of Pavlov (a great scientist, but no psychologist).

At home, every time you feed the fish, you turn on the light to the aquarium. They swim to the top to get the food. They swim to the top because food is there. Pair the light with the food often enough, and they learn to swim to the top when you turn on the aquarium light, even when no food is presented.

Watson, an actual psychologist, showed a baby, " Little Albert" a white rat. Little Albert liked the rat. Then Watson started banging a pipe whenever the white rat appeared. Soon, Little Albert feared the rat because the presentation of the rat had been paired with a loud sound so often. Sound or not, Little Albert cried whenever that rat appeared. This too was classical conditioning.

Every time you sit in the dentist's chair, she pokes you and hurts you. One day, you sit in her chair just to talk, no procedures performed. You are anxious, why? Classical conditioning. The chair had been paired so many times with unpleasantness, you feel anxious just sitting in the thing.

The author has nothing against dentists. They are good folks. Pavlov and Watson discovered something important insofar as classical conditioning is concerned. The author, however, has wondered for some time Little Albert holds a grudge against Watson.

30
THE WHOLE THING

Ever hear the phrase " The Whole is greater than the sum of its parts?" This phrase comes from psychology, a field of psychology called Gestalt psychology. What this phrase means is that we perceive things in whole, and then notice its parts. We see an object as a bird, and then we notice it has a red beak and blue feathers. By the way, the phrase " The Whole is greater than the sum of its parts" is true, but it is a misquote. What was actually said was " The whole is other than the sum of its parts."

31
WEIRD PSYCHOLOGY AND THE WESTERN WORLD

An interesting, and valid criticism of psychology is that it is, for the most part, weird.

What exactly do we mean? Most researchers, research subjects, and psychologists are weird. Let me explain. By weird I mean:
Western
Educated (people from...)
Industrialized
Rich
Democratic countries.

Indeed, the field of psychology is very weird.

32
FEAR OF LOSS

Often, psychology finds itself teaming up with other disciplines. Such is the case with Dr. Daniel Kahneman, a Nobel Prize winner in Economics. Dr. Kahneman discovered that people fear loss much more than they appreciate and enjoy gain. Often, to understand human behavior, contributions from experts outside of psychology are important. The field of Economics has made many contributions to the study of human behavior.

33
DIAGNOSING AUTISM

We know that people are being diagnosed more frequently with Autism. Is this due to better diagnostic techniques or an actual increase in the disorder? It is now referred to as Autism Spectrum Disorder. Meaning you can have very few symptoms that are almost unnoticeable, or very severe symptoms that impact your ability to function. You fall somewhere on a wide spectrum.

Why are numbers increasing? We do not know for sure, but there are a lot of theories: illness of the mother during pregnancy, age of the father at conception, pollution, and on and on. Is it one affliction, or several that seem similar? One thing for sure, answers will be found. Science always progresses.

Until recently, imaging of the brain, blood tests, genetic tests, etc. were not used in diagnosing autism. So diagnosis was clinical judgment, rarely possible before the age of two, as Autism is a social disorder.

Gains are being made in treatment and diagnosis. Often diagnosis and treatment are an art and a science in the beginning stages, and becomes mostly science as progress is made in diagnosis and treatment.

Just as AIDS once seemed unsolvable, and now is viewed as a chronic but treatable disease due to scientific research, it is very likely that Autism Spectrum Disorder will see similar breakthroughs

34
STOCKHOLM SYNDROME

Here's one a lot of folks have heard about: Stockholm Syndrome. This was a perennial favorite of the author's Introduction to Psychology students.

Stockholm syndrome is a psychological response wherein a captive begins to identify closely with his or her captors, as well as with their agenda and demands.

The name of the syndrome is derived from a botched bank robbery in Stockholm, Sweden. In August 1973 four employees of Sveriges Kreditbank were held hostage in the bank's vault for six days. During the standoff, a seemingly odd bond developed between captive and captor. One hostage, during a telephone call with Swedish Prime Minister Olof Palme, stated that she fully trusted her captors but feared that she would die in a police assault on the bank.

The most infamous example of Stockholm syndrome may be that involving kidnapped newspaper heiress Patricia Hearst. In 1974, some 10 weeks after being taken hostage by the Symbionese Liberation Army, Hearst helped her kidnappers rob a California bank. But it was during the hostage crisis in Iran(1979–81) that the Stockholm syndrome worked its way into the public imagination. The syndrome was also cited after the 1985 hijacking of TWA flight 847. Although passengers underwent a hostage ordeal that stretched more than two weeks, upon their release some were openly sympathetic to the demands of their kidnappers.

Terry Anderson (1985–91), Terry Waite (1987–91), and Thomas Sutherland (1985–91), all of whom had been kidnapped by Islamist militants in Lebanon, claimed that they had been treated well by their captors, despite the fact that they had often been held in solitary confinement and chained up in small, unclean cells. The hostages held at the Japanese embassy in Peru in 1996–97, exhibited similar responses.

Psychologists who have studied the syndrome believe that the bond is initially created when a captor threatens a captive's life, deliberates, and then chooses not to kill the captive. The captive's relief at the removal of the death threat is transposed into feelings of gratitude toward the captor for giving him or her life. As the Stockholm bank robbery incident proves, it takes only a few days for this bond to cement, proving that, early on, the victim's desire to survive trumps the urge to hate the person who created the situation.

The survival instinct is at the heart of the Stockholm
syndrome. Victims live in enforced dependence and interpret
rare or small acts of kindness in the midst of horrible
conditions as good treatment. They often become hyper
vigilant to the needs and demands of their captors, making
psychological links between the captors' happiness and their
own. Indeed, not only a positive bond between captive and
captor marks the syndrome but also by a negative attitude
on behalf of the captive toward authorities who threaten the
captor-captive relationship.

The negative attitude is especially powerful when the
hostage is of no use to the captors except as leverage
against a third party, as has often been the case with
political hostages.

By the 21st century, psychologists had expanded their understanding of the Stockholm syndrome from hostages to other groups, including victims of domestic violence, cult members, prisoners of war, procured prostitutes, and abused children. The American Psychiatric Association does not include Stockholm syndrome in its Diagnostic and Statistical Manual of Mental Disorders (DSM).

Now here is perhaps the most interesting part. Evolutionary psychologists theorize that Stockholm syndrome probably evolved from the early days of humans. When we were hunter-gatherers early humans frequently abducted members of other tribes. To avoid death, those abducted went along with it.

Now you know why you like the boss?

35
TALK ABOUT IT WHEN YOU'VE DONE IT

Want to loose that weight, finish school, finally read that book.
If we tell everyone we are going to do those things, and keep
telling them, we often feel that talking about doing something a
lot is enough. We become satisfied with having talked about it
a lot, so we do not actually go out and do it. Sometimes our
brain substitutes thinking for doing.

I am going to cut that grass, believe me everyone; I am going to
do it.

36
CHOOSE YOUR FONT WISELY

Research has shown some fonts are better received than others. Some are viewed as being trustworthier than others. When there is printing on a piece of candy, how we rate the taste is, in part, dependent on the font used.

We tend to attach meaning to shapes and appearances.

37
SLEEP

Sleep is tremendously important. When we experience deep sleep memories are consolidated. If we do not get enough sleep we are more likely to suffer from a variety of physical and mental disorders. We are also more likely to gain weight.

Poor judgment and poor reflexes during the day are caused by sleep deprivation.

People that were sleep derived caused some recent history: Chernobyl, Three Mile Island, and the Challenger disaster are just some of the examples.

Get some rest.

38
POLITICS DOESN'T ADD UP

Our political beliefs impact our ability to solve problems, especially math problems. Pro Gun control Democrats made a lot of errors in math when they were asked to crunch data that disagreed with their beliefs on the issue.

Republicans also made errors when working with data that conflicted with their beliefs.

Any surprises here?

39
MUSIC SOOTHES

Tourette Syndrome is a neurological disorder that involves not only tics, but in some cases involuntary swearing and offensive language from the person that suffers from the disorder.

Music can often bring the inappropriate outbursts and tics under control. It is not known why.

40
JUMPING LUMBERJACKS!

Chalk this one up as an odd rarity. A very rare psychological disorder exists among Lumberjacks of French-Canadian descent in New England (themselves a rare personage). When surprised or startled, they will jump, wave their arms about, and throw things. This rare disorder is called the " Jumping Frenchman of Maine Syndrome".

The author worked many years as a Psychologist, and never saw this one. Full disclosure: I have never set foot in Maine. It is not because of a fear of Jumping Frenchman, just a lack of opportunity. I do, however, enjoy lobster.

41
MY BRAINS EXPLODING!

About twenty percent of college students suffer from
" Exploding Head Syndrome" late at night when they are
attempting to go to sleep.   This involves an auditory
hallucination that may take the form of music, a siren, a bell, or
even a gunshot. We do not know why this is the case.
When I lived in a college dorm I just thought some of the
residents were playing music very late to make it difficult for
me to get to sleep. Maybe my head was exploding.

We do not know why this occurs. Though it is theorized that
some brains just have a bit of trouble "powering down" at that
age.

42
I AM THE WALRUS, COO COO CACHOO

There are historical cases of a disorder called Zoanthropy. This involves someone believing that they are an animal. A specific type of this disorder, Boanthropy, involves people that believe they are Cows or Oxen.

Again, a disorder I have never come across.

The Bible (Daniel 4:33) suggests Nebuchadnezzar II may have suffered from this. " He was driven from men and did eat grass as Oxen".

I had a Dachshund like this, but she thought she was human.

43
BE CAREFUL IN THE HOLY LAND

A very small percentage of visitors to the Holy Land succumb
to " Jerusalem Syndrome".

Those afflicted will do things such as wander around in robes
made of bed sheets, deliver extemporaneous sermons at the
Holy sites, and even wander the desert. Some believe they are
the Messiah.

44
BRAGADOCIOUS

Science knows why people like to talk about themselves. A little braggadocios rhetoric fires up the " pleasure center " of the brain. (So do money, sex, and food). Many folks will even pass up opportunities for money to talk about themselves.

The President must be a happy man. Probably not, he has said he is the most humble man in the world.

45
LIBERAL AND CONSERVATIVE PROBLEM SOLVING

Those that identify as liberal tend to solve problems differently than folks that identify as conservative. Even when solving problems that are clearly non-political.

Liberals tend to favor insight over analysis, whereby conservatives use intuitive insight and logical analysis.

A comparison of FDR to Reagan brings this in light.

46
TAKE A NAP

Taking naps during the day makes people more resilient and less impulsive. Many progressive companies have installed " Nap pods" on their corporate campuses.

Over the years, my college students seemed to grasp the importance of napping even before I lectured about it. They would nap during my lectures.

47
SWITCHT TRACKING

Often, when you argue with someone one of you will engage in "switchtracking".

In a heated argument, someone that begins arguing about *how* you are arguing, is employing this technique.

Someone that employs switchtracking is attempting to steer the conversation to ground they are more comfortable with.

The name comes from railroads when trains can shift quickly form one track to another with the flip of a switch.

48
HEARTACHE

Our brain reacts to social rejection, especially rejection by someone that means a lot to us, the same way it reacts to physical pain. Oddly enough, for some folks, acetaminophen can help with both kinds of pain.

49
THEY ARE PLAYING MY SONG

Hearing songs "in your head" that are really not playing in the environment is not uncommon. Past experiences, even extremely old ones, can sometimes prompt us to hear music that is not there.

50
MY HALO

First impressions are important, they color all subsequent impressions.

If someone makes a good first impression, you are quite likely to judge his or her future actions in a positive way. Psychologists call this the " Halo Effect".

This is why appearance is important. It is usually the first impression that we have of someone.

51
URINALS, AIM WELL

Go to an airport, a restaurant, or any place of business with restrooms and you soon notice a lot of men miss when they are relieving themselves. Sometimes, there is quite the yellow river on the floor.

A janitor at the airport in Amsterdam came up with a solution. He put a decal of a fly (realistic looking) in the urinal, so men had a target.

Virtually all of the" splashback" was eliminated.

Nobel anyone?

52
YIPS!

How does an accomplished professional gofer loose it? The Yips. To get to a high level of proficiency in a professional sport, thousands of hours of practice are required. So much practice, in fact, "muscle memory" takes over. You do not have to think about your swing, you just swing. In a high-pressure situation, you begin to think about your swing, over think about it. This is called the Yips.

Parallels exist in baseball: the catcher that cannot throw the ball back to the pitcher without throwing it over his head.

The yips are so feared no one speaks of them.

Most professional teams at the highest levels now employ sports psychologists.

53
GASLIGHTING

Gaslighting is a tactic in which a person or entity, in order to gain more power, makes a victim question their reality. It works much better than you may think. Anyone is susceptible to gaslighting, and it is a common technique of abusers, dictators, narcissists, and cult leaders. It is done slowly, so the victim doesn't realize how much they've been brainwashed. For example, in the movie _Gaslight_ (1944), a man manipulates his wife to the point where she thinks she is losing her mind.

People whom gaslight typically use the following techniques:

1. They tell blatant lies.
You know it's an outright lie. Yet they are telling you this lie with a straight face. Why are they so blatant? Because they're setting up a precedent. Once they tell you a huge lie, you're not sure if anything they say is true. Keeping you unsteady and off-kilter is the goal.
2. They deny they ever said something, even though you have proof.
You know they said they would do something; you know you heard it. But they out and out deny it. It makes you start questioning your reality—maybe they never said that thing. And the more they do this, the more you question your reality and start accepting theirs.
3. They use what is near and dear to you as ammunition.
They know how important your kids are to you, and they know how important your _identity_ is to you. So those may be

one of the first things they attack. If you have kids, they tell you that you should not have had those children. They will tell you'd be a worthy person if only you didn't have a long list of negative traits. They attack the foundation of your being.

4. They wear you down over time.
This is one of the insidious things about gaslighting—it is done gradually, over time. A lie here, a lie there, and a snide comment every so often...and then it starts ramping up. Even the brightest, most self-aware people can be sucked into gaslighting—it is that effective. It's the "frog in the frying pan" analogy: The heat is turned up slowly, so the frog never realizes what's happening to it.
5. Their actions do not match their words.
When dealing with a person or entity that gaslights, look at what they are doing rather than what they are saying. What they are saying means nothing; it is just talk. What they are doing is the issue.
6. They throw in positive reinforcement to confuse you.
This person or entity that is <u>cutting</u> you down, telling you that you don't have value, is now praising you for something you did. This adds an additional sense of uneasiness. You think, "Well maybe they aren't so bad." Yes, they are. This is a calculated attempt to keep you off-kilter—and again, to question your reality. Also look at what you were praised for; it is probably something that served the gaslighter.

7. They know confusion weakens people.
Gaslighters know that people like having a sense of stability and normalcy. Their goal is to uproot this and

make you constantly question everything. And humans' natural tendency is to look to the person or entity that will help you feel more stable—and that happens to be the gaslighter.

8. They project.
They are a drug user or a cheater, yet they are constantly accusing you of that. This is done so often that you start trying to defend yourself, and are distracted from the gaslighter's own behavior.
9. They try to align people against you.
Gaslighters are masters at manipulating and finding the people they know will stand by them no matter what—and they use these people against you. They will make comments such as, "This person knows that you're not right," or "This person knows you're useless too." Keep in mind it does not mean that these people actually said these things. A gaslighter is a constant liar. When the gaslighter uses this tactic it makes you feel like you don't know who to trust or turn to—and that leads you right back to the gaslighter. And that's exactly what they want: Isolation gives them more control.

54
BLONDES HAVE MORE FUN?

When many people think of blondes the terms like bubbly, sexy, dumb, fun, hot, and ditzy come to mind along with a few others. In fact, each hair color has its stereotypes. The Redhead: passionate, fiery, and seductive. The Brunette: stable, boring, elegant, and smart. Black hair: mysterious, rebellious, sultry, tough. But the question is does your hair color really affect how you act or how others perceive or treat you?

Many of us have heard that men like blondes compared to any other hair color. But is this true? Research from Florida State University has shown that men prefer women with long brown hair to anything else. Of the men polled, 46% preferred women with brown hair, 27% preferred black, 19% preferred blondes, and only 7% preferred redheads (if you are a redhead, don't fret. Research shows that red-haired women have more sex than brunettes or blondes.).
Another study in Paris found that blondes can actually make the people around them dumber. Researchers found that men's scores on general knowledge tests drop when they are shown photos of blonde women. Professor Thierry Meyer, joint author of the study published in the Journal of Experimental Psychology, said, "It proves that people confronted with stereotypes generally behave in line with them. Blondes have the potential to make people act in a dumber way, because they mimic the unconscious stereotype of the dumb blonde."
But the question stands, do blondes really have more fun? This study thinks so and it all has to do with the increased confidence being blonde gives the person. The research,

commissioned by the hair care company, Clairol, found that females who dyed their hair in blonde shades enjoyed increased confidence in themselves and their abilities at work. In addition to women feeling differently towards themselves, they also feel men treat them differently. Sergeant stated that

Women believe "if you dye your hair red, most men see you as being fiery. If you dye your hair blonde, men see you as bubbly and fun."
So, what do you think? Do blondes have more fun? Does having your hair a certain shade really change your personality?

55
SUPERHEROES

Why do kids like Superman, the Hulk, Spider-Man, Batman, Thor, Wolverine, the Incredibles family, Captain America – and all the other superheroes so popular today? It's simple, says Axel Alonso. He's Editor-in-Chief at Marvel Comics. "Kids need heroes," he says. "While parents should be role models for life, superheroes remind a child of the moral compass necessary to navigate a universe fraught with thrills and danger."